Roald
DAHL

Roald
DAHL

by Chris Powling

🍂 Carolrhoda Books, Inc. / Minneapolis

Carolrhoda Books, Inc., c/o The Lerner Publishing Group
241 First Avenue North, Minneapolis, Minnesota 55401 U.S.A.

Website address: www.lernerbooks.com

Library of Congress Cataloging-in-Publication Data

Powling, Chris.
  Roald Dahl / Chris Powling.
    p. cm. — (Tell me about)
  Includes index.
  Summary: A brief biography of the writer of such successful books as "Charlie and the Chocolate Factory," "James and the Giant Peach," and "Matilda."
  ISBN 1–57505–274–1 (alk. paper)
  1. Dahl, Roald—Juvenile literature. 2. Authors, English—20th century—Biography—Juvenile literature. 3. Children's stories—Authorship—Juvenile literature. [1. Dahl, Roald. 2. Authors, English.] I. Title. II. Series: Tell me about (Minneapolis, Minn.)
PR6054.A35Z84   1998
823'.914—dc21
  [B]   97–33403
Printed by Graficas Reunidas SA, Spain
Bound in the United States of America
1 2 3 4 5 6 – OS – 03 02 01 00 99 98

Have you heard of Fantastic Mr. Fox? Or read about the Enormous Crocodile? Do you know what was so scary about the Magic Finger? If you answered yes, then you are probably a fan of Roald Dahl already. If you said no, don't worry—it means you are in for a treat! That's because Roald Dahl was one of the most successful and popular children's authors ever. This is his story.

Roald Dahl in his writing hut

When Roald Dahl died, in November 1990, the eighteen books of stories and rhymes he wrote for young people had sold millions of copies all over the world. His books are still just as popular as when he was alive. There is even a special Roald Dahl museum that you can visit. It is in Aylesbury, England, near where he lived.

Making a model (above) and having fun (left and right) at the Roald Dahl Museum in Aylesbury, England

You can see his stories on the screen and on video, in movies such as *Willy Wonka and the Chocolate Factory, James and the Giant Peach,* and *Matilda.*

Yes, Roald Dahl was a scrumdiddlyumptious storyteller!

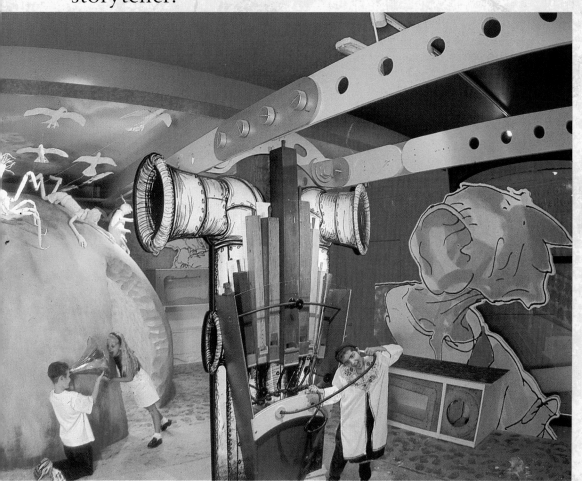

Roald's own life was almost as strange and exciting as some of his stories. He wrote about his life in *Boy* and *Going Solo*. These books show that he was always a bit of an outsider, someone who never acted the way he was expected to.

(Above) Roald grew orchids as a hobby. (Left) A notice on the board says one of his orchids won first prize.

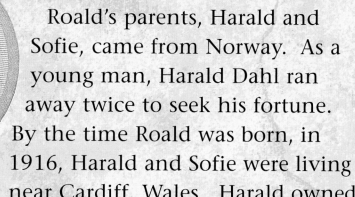

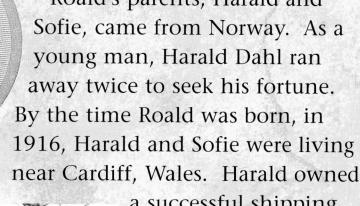

Roald's father, Harald

Roald's parents, Harald and Sofie, came from Norway. As a young man, Harald Dahl ran away twice to seek his fortune. By the time Roald was born, in 1916, Harald and Sofie were living near Cardiff, Wales. Harald owned a successful shipping business there. Harald died in 1920, so it was Sofie who brought Roald up. The family lived in a house called Cumberland Lodge. Roald was very close to his mother.

Roald and his mother, Sofie

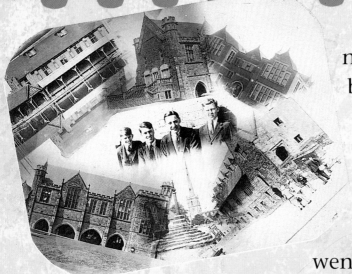

When Roald was nine, he went to boarding school. He didn't like it much. He wanted to seek his own fortune. After he left school, he went to work in Africa.

Some photographs that Roald took while at boarding school

Roald in Africa

When World War II began in 1939, Roald decided to join Britain's Royal Air Force as a pilot. Being a pilot was exciting, but also dangerous. Roald's plane crashed in the desert in Libya. Roald was badly hurt in the crash and walked with a limp for the rest of his life.

This is a painting of Roald by the artist Matthew Smith. Roald collected modern art.

In 1942, Roald went to the United States to work for the British government. While he was there, he wrote a story about his adventures as a pilot. It was published in an important magazine. Roald began writing more stories for adults and for children. Walt Disney wanted to make one story, "The Gremlins," into a movie.

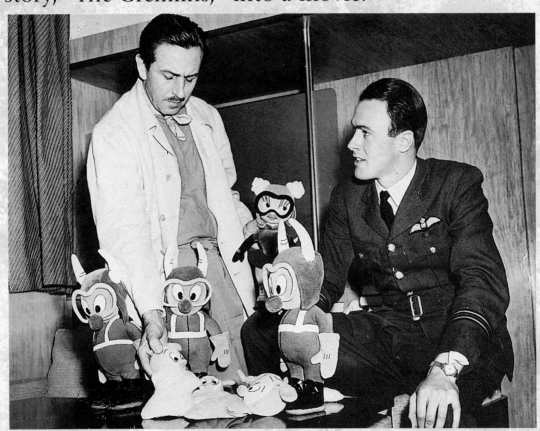

Roald with Walt Disney and the Gremlins

The movie was never made, but Roald's career as a writer had begun. After the war, he lived partly in England and partly in America. In 1953, he married an American movie star, Patricia Neal. They bought a farmhouse called Gipsy House in a small village in England. They had five children —Olivia, Tessa, Theo, Ophelia, and Lucy.

Roald
and
Patricia

Gipsy
House

Roald and his family went through some hard times in the early 1960s. First, Theo's baby carriage was hit by a taxi in New York City. Theo was thrown from the carriage and his brain was badly damaged. Roald wanted to help Theo recover. With a doctor and an engineer, Roald invented a special device called the Wade-Dahl-Till valve. It helped children with brain injuries. Luckily, Theo got better by himself, but the valve saved the lives of thousands of children.

Theo Dahl as a child

Something even worse happened in 1962. Roald's daughter Olivia died of a rare type of measles. If you read *The BFG*, you will see that it has a special dedication to Olivia.

The Dahl family's troubles were still not over. Roald's wife Patricia had a stroke, a serious illness. To help her recover, Roald kept her busy. He brought friends and neighbors to talk and play games with her every day. After almost three years, she was well enough to make movies again.

ROALD DAHL

The BFG

Illustrated by

QUENTIN BLAKE

For Olivia

20 April 1955 — 17 November 1962

Olivia, Patricia, and Tessa

Amazingly, while these terrible things were happening, Roald was becoming more and more successful as a children's author. His first stories were based on bedtime tales he told his own children. He did his writing in a shed at Gipsy House.

Roald's writing hut *(right)* and a picture he took of Dylan Thomas's writing hut. Roald loved Thomas's poetry.

When Roald was writing, he would settle down in an old armchair with a wooden board propped across it. Then he would sharpen six yellow pencils. He would write for hours, wearing out the pencils. "One of the nice things about being a writer," he once said, "is that all you need is what you've got in your head and a pencil and a bit of paper."

Inside Roald's hut

George's Marvellous Medicine
Illustrated by
QUENTIN BLAKE

What did Roald have in his head? *The Twits*, and *George's Marvelous Medicine*, and *Esio Trot*, and *The Minpins*, and *The Giraffe and the Pelly and Me*, and more. Slowly, steadily, Roald's books made him one of the most famous and successful writers for children ever.

Not everyone loved his books, though. In fact, plenty of grown-ups did not like his writing at all, and still don't. "He's too rude," they complain. "He appeals only to the bad side of children. His stories won't make them better people."

You can make up your own mind about Roald's stories.

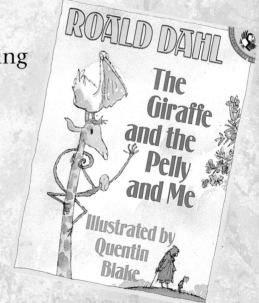

ROALD DAHL
The Giraffe and the Pelly and Me
Illustrated by Quentin Blake

Several of Roald Dahl's books have pictures by Quentin Blake. Blake based the drawings for *The BFG* (which stands for Big Friendly Giant) on Roald himself.

A model of the BFG for the Dahl Museum

Quentin Blake and Roald Dahl at work at Gipsy House

Roald died in 1990. After his death, his second wife, Felicity, set up the Roald Dahl Foundation.

Roald with his son, Theo, and some young friends

This charity helps children and adults with serious illness and with problems with reading and writing. Roald would have loved this. He once said, "I suppose I could knock at the door of any house where there was a child—whether it was in the US, Britain, Holland, Germany, France—and say, 'My car's run out of petrol (gas). Could you please give me a cup of tea?' And they would know me. That does make me feel good!"

To feel good yourself, read one of his stories!

Important Dates

1916 Roald Dahl born in Cardiff, Wales

1925 Sent to boarding school

1938 Moved to Africa while working for the Shell Oil Company

1939 Joined the Royal Air Force as a pilot

1940 Plane crashed over Libya

1942 Went to the United States to work for the British government. Wrote a story for the *Saturday Evening Post.*

1943 First book, *The Gremlins,* was published

1953 Married Patricia Neal

1960 Son, Theo, suffered a brain injury in an accident

1962 Daughter Olivia died

1965 Wife Patricia Neal had a stroke

1983 Divorced Patricia Neal. Married Felicity Crosland.

1988 Last book, *Matilda,* published

1990 Roald Dahl died at age 74

Index

Acknowledgments

The author and publisher gratefully acknowledge the following for permission to reproduce copyrighted material:
Cover Jan Baldwin **Title page** © Dahl Estate **page 5** Jan Baldwin **pages 6 and 7** © Bremner & Orr Design Consultants Ltd 1996 **page 8** (left) Jan Baldwin (right) Sanjiro Minamikawa/Martyn F. Chillmaid **page 9** © Dahl Estate **page 10** © Dahl Estate/Martyn F. Chillmaid **page 11** © Dahl Estate **page 12** © Dahl Estate/Martyn F. Chillmaid **page 13** (top) © Dahl Estate/Martyn F. Chillmaid (bottom) Jan Baldwin **page 14** © Dahl Estate **page 15** (left) © Dahl Estate/Martyn F. Chillmaid **page 16** (top) Jan Baldwin/Martyn F. Chillmaid (bottom) © Dahl Estate **page 17** Jan Baldwin **page 19** © Dahl Estate/Martyn F. Chillmaid **page 20** Leonard McComb/Martyn Chillmaid © Life Magazine **Back cover** © Dahl Estate

For more information about the Roald Dahl Museum and Foundation, write to the following address:

92 High Street
Great Missenden
Buckinghamshire HP16 0AN
United Kingdom

About the Author

In his native England, Chris Powling is the well-known author of more than 25 children's books. Some of his books, including *Hiccup Harry* and *The Phantom Car Wash,* have also been published in the United States. Mr. Powling studied education at Oxford, the University of London, and the University of Sussex, as well as speech and drama at the Royal Academy of Music. He is a former teacher and principal and now makes his living as a full-time writer. Mr. Powling lives in Greenwich, just outside London, with his wife and two daughters.